CRIMCOMICS

SOCIAL CONTROL THEORIES

KRISTA S. GEHRING

WRITER

MICHAEL R. BATISTA

ARTIST

CHERYL L. WALLACE

LETTERER

New York   Oxford

OXFORD UNIVERSITY PRESS

To Natalee,
I appreciate you and all your love and support.

—KRISTA S. GEHRING

To Robyn,
For being supportive of me and my creative work.

—MICHAEL R. BATISTA

FOREWORD

Students and teachers interested in juvenile delinquency and criminology are confronted with an enormous amount of research and data about the nature of crime, its distribution over time and place, the characteristics of offenders, and claims about the roles of families, peers, poverty, schools, demography, and social forces in fostering or inhibiting delinquency and crime. There is an additional large body of literature about the consequences of the juvenile justice and criminal justice systems, and the effects of the police, juvenile courts, and prisons—all of which can easily be overwhelming. Nearly daily we hear what seem to be conflicting conclusions about crime from the media, the police, schools, and scholars. Theories of crime, meant to offer clear perspective and understanding to the field, can seem strangely divorced from all the data, all of the media images, and the sincere desire to learn what is the best evidence and thinking about crime today.

In this context, the imaginative and creative innovation of *CrimComics* is a terrific new mechanism to help introduce and guide students through the challenges and satisfactions of many of the most important ideas (and the history of these ideas)

actively discussed in modern criminology. Few topics taught in colleges and universities have greater interest to students than does criminology—topics like violence, punishment, delinquency, white-collar crime, and substance abuse. Why is it that nearly everyone, sometimes—and some people, relatively often—harms others in order to get what they want? What causes these behaviors, and what can—or should—be done about them? Searching for answers to these questions is natural and has interested scholars from philosophy and literature to biology and sociology. Such questions involve fundamental issues about the human condition, about effectiveness and fairness of the institutions (such as law) that have been created to deal with crime; indeed, about the causes of social order. They are, in short, among the most fundamental and intriguing questions one can ask, and it is not surprising that they continue to intrigue scholars from a wide range of disciplines.

Questions such as these are complex, but the job of the theorist is to make them less complex; to tie things together that should go together; to explain why; and to offer clear, parsimonious, accurate, and satisfying answers. It is not surprising, given the importance of the questions, and the nearly ubiquitous fascination with the topic, that scholars have worked hard to develop accurate and satisfying explanations for delinquency and crime. Decades of research from the behavioral sciences has produced a body of very high quality information about crime and delinquency, research that sets the stage for seeking explanations to help us make sense of the complexity that these studies depict and to help guide further fact-finding. This is the role of theoretical criminology, today one of the most vibrant and exciting areas in the study of crime.

Given the importance of the questions and the large interest in finding answers, it is exciting to see Krista Gehring and Michael Batista create the innovative series *CrimComics*, a terrific new method to help us learn about and think more clearly about the theoretical traditions used today by behavioral scientists. They do so in a way that helps describe the intellectual roots of these ideas and helps provide guidance about areas that might be of further interest to readers. The scholarship underlying *CrimComics* is serious, and organizing it and presenting it as clearly as they do is a marvelous contribution to our field.

Theories are efforts to provide organization and simplification to all this complexity and the abundance of data and studies. A good theory will help bring order to the "findings" about crime and will in a straightforward and clear way explain why they occur and why they go together. Not only will a good theory be consistent with the facts, but it will also be logically consistent internally and yield predictions about the effects of juvenile and criminal justice that turn out also to be true. It will help guide research in the future and provide hints about what to expect from policy or programs. A good theory will help us understand why delinquency and crime happen and help us speculate about what can be done to minimize their occurrence. A good theory will spark the imagination and lead to the discovery of new, useful knowledge. Good theories should be parsimonious, they should be internally logical, they should attend to the most important facts in a field, and they should help predict facts not yet in evidence.

Theoretical criminology is a vibrant and challenging part of criminology, and learning about various perspectives and the reasons that they continue to be studied and developed can be an exciting and rewarding intellectual challenge, one with considerable real-world implications. In the end, the reduction of harms, both to victims and offenders, is the underlying idea that animates most theorists, an objective well worth pursuing. *CrimComics* will serve as a stimulating introduction to theoretical criminology and am sure that readers will find this presentation invaluable.

MICHAEL R. GOTTFREDSON
Chancellors' Professor, University of California, Irvine

PREFACE

The subject matter for this issue takes a departure from many of the previous issues that have discussed criminological theory. While those issues have focused on the question "Why do people commit crime?," social control theories ask a different question: "Why *don't* people commit crime?" Implicit in this inquiry is the assumption that crime and deviance are natural; that is, they will occur unless prevented by ties to conventional institutions and certain controls are put in place.

This is an interesting thought experiment. What if there were nothing in place to control our behavior? For example, what if there were no laws, no institutions of formal or informal control? Would there be anarchy, lawlessness, continual victimization? Or would humans conform anyway, regardless of the lack of controls?

What keeps *you* from committing crime? Are you afraid that you may lose your stake in conformity, such as a job or a relationship? Do you realize that if you commit crime, you would disappoint individuals who are important to you? Are you able to delay the short-term gratification of crime and put in the work for things you want? These and other circumstances illustrate aspects of social control, as social control theories posit that people's relationships, commitments, values, norms, and beliefs encourage them not to break the law. I encourage the readers of this issue to view these concepts in such a way to see how they apply to their personal circumstances, as many of the concepts will likely explain why they *don't* commit crime.

I would also encourage readers to ponder Travis Hirschi's impact on the development of control theory, as his contributions have been noteworthy and . . . interesting. In 1969, Hirschi published the work *Causes of Delinquency* in which he not only proposed his control theory (referred to as social bond theory), but he also challenged the two major paradigms at that time: Edwin Sutherland's differential association theory (which he referred to as cultural deviance theory) and Merton's strain theory. His goal was to start a theoretical fight, and this theoretical sparring became a hallmark of his career. Social bond theory proposed that the strength of four bonds (attachment, commitment, involvement, and belief) to social institutions could vary. Social bonds remain strong only so long as they are cultivated through interactions with conventional others. The stronger the bond, the less likely crime would occur. Therefore, the locus of control in this theory was external to the individual.

Two decades later, however, Hirschi appeared to change his tune. His work with Michael Gottfredson produced *A General Theory of Crime* (1990) in which they proposed self-control theory. This theory was related to his earlier theory, but it ultimately competes with it. In self-control theory, the locus of control shifts to an internal characteristic and its combination with criminal opportunity to generate crime. Hirschi himself states that this was a "modification" of control theory; however, the control concepts are very different when the two theories are compared. Indeed, John Laub pointed out that the "field has been struggling to reconcile" the two perspectives; however, this does not detract from the fact that Hirschi has dominated control theory for five decades by generating two of the most important control models of crime.

As with any book project, *CrimComics* consumed much time and effort, perhaps more so than a traditional textbook. Thinking about theory—and, in particular, trying to design a work that best conveys the theories in a visual medium—is fun. Still, with busy lives, finding the space in one's day to carefully research, write, illustrate, ink, and letter the pages of this work is a source of some stress. We were fortunate, however, to have had an amazing amount of support during these times from family, friends, and Oxford University Press. We also want to acknowledge the talents of Cheryl Wallace.

Cheryl's flair for lettering allowed us to get our ideas across to the readers.

The support of these and so many other individuals has made creating *CrimComics* possible and a rewarding experience for us. We would like to thank the following reviewers: Harold Wells, Tennessee State University; Viviana Andreescu, University of Louisville; Thomas Chuda, Bunker Hill Community College; Ellen Cohn, Florida International University; Robert Jenkot, Coastal Carolina University; Suman Kakar, Florida International University; Venezia Michalsen, Montclair State University; Paul Edward Nunis, Arkansas State University; Allison Ann Payne, Villanova University; Elizabeth B Perkins, Morehead State University; Sean Wilson, William Paterson University. We hope that this and other issues of *CrimComics* will inspire in your students a passion to learn criminological theory.

Social Control Theories

CHICAGO, 1925.

THEORIES THAT TRY TO EXPLAIN CRIMINAL BEHAVIOR TEND TO FOCUS ON ANSWERING THE QUESTION "WHY DO PEOPLE COMMIT CRIME?"

IMPLICIT IN THIS QUESTION IS THE BELIEF THAT IT IS NATURAL FOR PEOPLE TO CONFORM TO THE RULES OF SOCIETY.

STOP! THIEF!

BUT WHAT IF CONFORMITY IS NOT THE NATURAL STATE OF HUMAN BEINGS?

WHAT IF NONCONFORMITY, SUCH AS CRIME AND DELINQUENCY, IS TO BE EXPECTED WHEN SOCIAL CONTROLS ARE INEFFECTIVE OR NOT PRESENT?

IF CRIME IS GRATIFYING, WHY DON'T INDIVIDUALS JUST BREAK THE LAW ALL THE TIME?

VIEWED THIS WAY, SOME THEORISTS ARE NOT INTERESTED IN WHY PEOPLE ENGAGE IN CRIME--THEY ARE INTERESTED IN WHY THEY DON'T.

EVENIN', WALT.

THIS IS THE FOCUS OF *SOCIAL CONTROL THEORIES.*

SOCIAL CONTROL THEORIES MAINTAIN THAT EVERYONE HAS THE POTENTIAL TO VIOLATE THE LAW AND THAT MODERN SOCIETY PRESENTS MANY OPPORTUNITIES FOR ILLEGAL ACTIVITY.

PEOPLE OBEY THE LAW BECAUSE BEHAVIOR AND PASSIONS ARE BEING CONTROLLED BY INTERNAL AND/OR EXTERNAL FORCES.

THE PREMISE OF CONTROL THEORY IS SIMPLE: WHEN CONTROLS ARE PRESENT, CRIME DOES NOT OCCUR; WHEN CONTROLS ARE ABSENT, CRIME OFTEN OCCURS.

ALL RIGHT! NOW HEAR THIS! NONE OF YOU ARE LEAVING THIS PLACE UNTIL ENOUGH SHOTS ARE DONE TO MAKE THIS STACK OF DOUGH GO AWAY!

THEREFORE, UNLIKE MOST CRIMINOLOGICAL THEORIES THAT FOCUS ON WHY PEOPLE COMMIT CRIME, SOCIAL CONTROL THEORIES POSE A DIFFERENT QUESTION:

"WHY DO PEOPLE CONFORM?"

LOOKS LIKE YOU AND ME ARE THE ONLY ONES LEFT STANDIN', WALT.

YOU DIDN'T DO A SINGLE SHOT?

NAH. GOTTA STAY SHARP! I NEED TO GO WORK ON MY DISSERTATION.

FOR SOMEONE WITH THE LAST NAME "RECKLESS," YOU ARE ANYTHING BUT.

LATER...

Valois Valois CAFETERIA 'SEE YOUR FOOD'

DO YOU GENTLEMEN HAVE ROOM FOR A POOR, LOWLY DOCTORAL STUDENT?

OF COURSE, MY BOY! COME TALK WITH US ABOUT YOUR DISSERTATION!

WALTER RECKLESS STUDIED SOCIOLOGY AT THE UNIVERSITY OF CHICAGO.

WHILE HE WAS THERE, HE JOINED THE AMERICAN SOCIOLOGISTS ROBERT PARK AND ERNEST BURGESS* IN CONDUCTING OBSERVATIONAL STUDIES OF CRIME IN CHICAGO.

ROBERT PARK

ERNEST BURGESS

IT HAPPENED AGAIN TONIGHT--CAPONE SHOWED UP!

I CAN'T BELIEVE THE LUCK I'M HAVING WHILE I'M GATHERING THIS DATA!

RECKLESS'S TIME AT THE UNIVERSITY OF CHICAGO EXPOSED HIM TO THE CHICAGO SCHOOL OF CRIMINOLOGY.

THIS SCHOOL'S THEORIES DIFFERED FROM THE DOMINANT THEORIES AT THE TIME. IT PROPOSED THAT CRIME WAS CAUSED BY SOCIAL FACTORS, NOT BIOLOGICAL OR PSYCHOLOGICAL DEFECTS.

Valois

RECKLESS GRAVITATED TOWARD THE IDEAS OF SOCIAL PSYCHOLOGY THAT MANY CHICAGO THEORISTS WERE USING TO EXPLAIN CRIMINAL BEHAVIOR AT THAT TIME.

THIS BELIEF IN SOCIOLOGICAL EXPLANATIONS OF BEHAVIOR WOULD BE ONE OF MANY INFLUENCES ON THE THEORY RECKLESS WOULD DEVELOP MANY YEARS LATER.

*LEARN MORE IN CRIMCOMICS: SOCIAL DISORGANIZATION THEORY!

TWENTY YEARS LATER.

AFTER WORLD WAR II, SOLDIERS RETURNED HOME AND STARTED FAMILIES, A TREND THAT WOULD EVENTUALLY TURN INTO THE **BABY BOOM.**

AMERICA TRANSITIONED INTO A PERIOD OF AFFLUENCE. IT ALSO MARKED THE BEGINNING OF SUBURBANIZATION.

UP TO THAT POINT, CRIMINOLOGISTS WERE CONCERNED WITH THE STUDY OF IMMIGRANTS IN THE INNER CITY (I.E., THE CHICAGO SCHOOL).

HOWEVER, CRIMINOLOGY STARTED TO TURN AWAY FROM THE STUDY OF IMMIGRANTS TO THE STUDY OF YOUTH, WHO WERE NOW CREATING A VIBRANT YOUTH CULTURE.

AND ALTHOUGH OTHER THEORISTS AT THE TIME WERE VERY MUCH INTERESTED IN DELINQUENT GANGS LOCATED IN INNER CITIES,* MANY OF THESE YOUTH WERE WHITE AND NOT LIVING IN THE SLUMS.

THEREFORE, WHEN IDEAS ASSOCIATED WITH CONTROL THEORIES EMERGED AT THIS TIME, THE THRUST WAS THAT SOCIAL CLASS WAS NOT A STRONG PREDICTOR OF CRIME AND THAT DELINQUENTS WERE NOT THAT MUCH DIFFERENT FROM "THE REST OF US."

*CHECK OUT CRIMCOMICS: SUBCULTURAL THEORIES FOR MORE!

DELINQUENTS THUS WERE NOT JACK-ROLLERS* BUT JOY-RIDERS...

...NOT POLISH IMMIGRANTS IN GANGS STEALING AND FIGHTING IN CHICAGO BUT HIGH SCHOOL KIDS SHOPLIFTING AND DRINKING.

THE OHIO STATE UNIVERSITY, 1960.

THE OHIO STATE UNIVERSITY

MANY YEARS LATER, RECKLESS WAS A PROFESSOR AT THE OHIO STATE UNIVERSITY.

IT WAS HERE HE REALLY BEGAN TO FORMULATE HIS CONTROL THEORY...

WHY DON'T ALL CHILDREN RAISED IN BAD ENVIRONMENTS BECOME DELINQUENT?

WHY DO CHILDREN RAISED IN GOOD ENVIRONMENTS BECOME DELINQUENT?

RECKLESS

*"JACK-ROLLER" REFERS TO A TEXT CLIFFORD SHAW WROTE IN 1930 THAT WAS AN AUTOBIOGRAPHY OF A DELINQUENT.

THE IDEAS THAT REALLY GOT RECKLESS THINKING HAD BEEN PUT FORTH BY SEVERAL CRIMINOLOGISTS REGARDING THE CONCEPT OF CONTROL:

REISS

ALBERT J. REISS WROTE "DELINQUENCY AS THE FAILURE OF PERSONAL AND SOCIAL CONTROLS" IN 1951.

TOBY

JACKSON TOBY INTRODUCED THE CONCEPT OF STAKES IN CONFORMITY IN 1957.

F. IVAN NYE EXPANDED SOCIAL CONTROL THEORY BY IDENTIFYING DIRECT CONTROL, INDIRECT CONTROL, INTERNALIZED CONTROL, AND AVAILABILITY OF NEED SATISFACTION (OPPORTUNITY CONTROL).

CLACK
CLACK

BUILDING UPON THESE AND OTHER IDEAS ABOUT SOCIAL CONTROL, WALTER RECKLESS DEVELOPED HIS *CONTAINMENT THEORY* IN THE EARLY 1960S.

IT FOCUSES ON AN INNER CONTROL SYSTEM AND AN OUTER CONTROL SYSTEM.

ACCORDING TO THIS THEORY, THERE ARE INNER AND OUTER *PUSHES* AND *PULLS* THAT MAY PRODUCE DELINQUENCY UNLESS THEY ARE CONSTRAINED OR COUNTERACTED BY INNER AND OUTER CONTAINMENT MEASURES.

HEY, DID YOU HEAR ABOUT THAT NEW COMIC THAT'S OUT? THE AMAZING SPIDER-MAN?

YEAH! IT'S SPIDER-MAN AND THE FANTASTIC FOUR!

A VARIETY OF FACTORS (E.G., BIOPHYSICAL FORCES, PSYCHOLOGICAL PRESSURES, SOCIAL CONDITIONS SUCH AS POVERTY) MIGHT "PUSH" A PERSON TOWARD CRIME OR DELINQUENCY.

I WISH I HADN'T SPENT MY LAST DIME ON THIS CHERRY COKE, OR I COULD GET IT!

OTHER FACTORS (E.G., ILLEGITIMATE OPPORTUNITIES) MIGHT "PULL" ONE TOWARD MISBEHAVIOR.

OUTER CONTAINMENT IS THE SOCIAL ENVIRONMENT IN WHICH THE INDIVIDUAL LIVES AND REFLECTS COMMUNITY SOCIALIZATION.

INNER CONTAINMENT CONTROLS THE INDIVIDUAL NO MATTER HOW THE EXTERNAL ENVIRONMENT MAY CHANGE. KEY FACTORS HERE ARE *SELF-CONCEPT, GOAL ORIENTATION, FRUSTRATION TOLERANCE*, AND *NORM RETENTION*.

FOR RECKLESS, HOWEVER, THE EMPHASIS WAS ON INNER CONTAINMENT.

I GUESS I'LL JUST HAVE TO SAVE UP MY ALLOWANCE AND HOPE THAT IT'S STILL ON THE RACK HERE NEXT WEEK

RECKLESS'S CONTAINMENT THEORY WAS MEANT TO EXPLAIN WHY IN SPITE OF THE VARIOUS PUSHES AND PULLS AN INDIVIDUAL MIGHT EXPERIENCE, CONFORMITY REMAINS THE GENERAL STATE OF BEING.

OR... I HAVE AN IDEA.

COMMITTING CRIME REQUIRES A PERSON TO BREAK THROUGH BOTH INNER AND OUTER CONTAINMENT THAT TEND TO INSULATE HIM OR HER FROM BOTH PUSHES AND PULLS.

FOR MOST PEOPLE, THIS RARELY OCCURS, BUT THIS EXPLAINS WHY SOME PEOPLE COMMITTED CRIME AND OTHERS DID NOT, REGARDLESS OF THEIR ENVIRONMENT.

TIMMY! WHAT ARE YOU DOING?

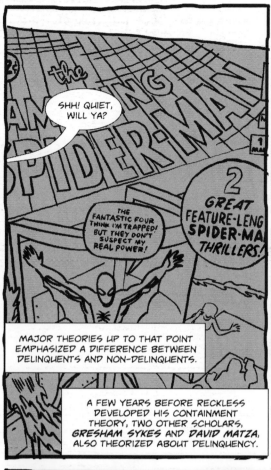

SHH! QUIET, WILL YA?

THE FANTASTIC FOUR THINK I'M TRAPPED! BUT THEY DON'T SUSPECT MY REAL POWER!

MAJOR THEORIES UP TO THAT POINT EMPHASIZED A DIFFERENCE BETWEEN DELINQUENTS AND NON-DELINQUENTS.

A FEW YEARS BEFORE RECKLESS DEVELOPED HIS CONTAINMENT THEORY, TWO OTHER SCHOLARS, **GRESHAM SYKES** AND **DAVID MATZA**, ALSO THEORIZED ABOUT DELINQUENCY.

SYKES AND MATZA ARGUED THAT DELINQUENTS RETAINED A COMMITMENT TO CONVENTIONAL SOCIETY AND ITS EXPECTATIONS.

THEY KNEW RIGHT FROM WRONG.

THEY ALSO ARGUED THAT YOUTHS COULD ENGAGE IN DELINQUENCY IF THEY COULD "ESCAPE" THE CONTROL THAT CONVENTIONAL SOCIETY HAD OVER THEM.

SYKES AND MATZA (1957) PROPOSED THERE WERE *TECHNIQUES OF NEUTRALIZATION* THAT PEOPLE USE TO JUSTIFY THEIR WRONGDOING TO THEMSELVES AND OTHERS.

THESE TECHNIQUES "NEUTRALIZE" THEIR VALUES TEMPORARILY SO THAT THEY CAN COMMIT ACTS THAT THEIR VALUES WOULD NOT OTHERWISE PERMIT.

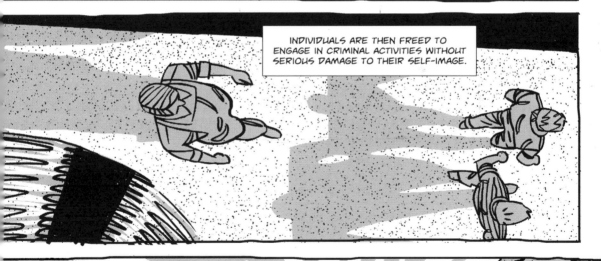

INDIVIDUALS ARE THEN FREED TO ENGAGE IN CRIMINAL ACTIVITIES WITHOUT SERIOUS DAMAGE TO THEIR SELF-IMAGE.

WHERE DO YOU THINK YOU ARE GOING?

GRAB

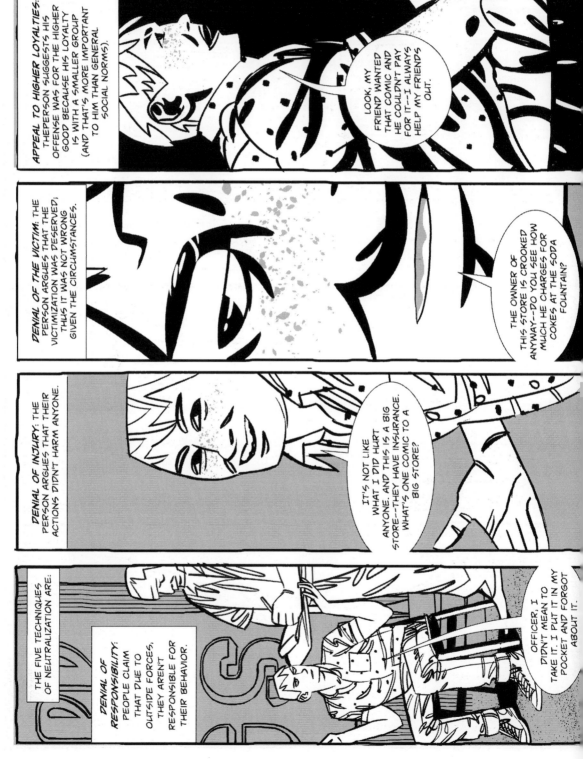

CONDEMNATION OF THE CONDEMNERS: THE PERSON MAY SHIFT THE FOCUS FROM HIS DELINQUENT ACT TO THE MOTIVES AND BEHAVIORS OF THOSE WHO DISAPPROVE OF THE BEHAVIOR.

C'MON. YOU KNOW YOU DID STUFF LIKE THIS WHEN YOU WERE A KID. EVERYONE STEALS--WHY ARE YOU PICKING ON ME?

YOU KNOW, COPS ARE CORRUPT TOO--I CAN'T BELIEVE YOU ARE BUSTING ME FOR THIS WHEN POLICE AND JUDGES HAVE DONE WAY WORSE.

APPEAL TO HIGHER LOYALTIES: THE PERSON SUGGESTS HIS OFFENSE WAS FOR THE HIGHER GOOD BECAUSE HIS LOYALTY IS WITH A SMALLER GROUP (AND THAT'S MORE IMPORTANT TO HIM THAN GENERAL SOCIAL NORMS).

LOOK, MY FRIEND WANTED THAT COMIC AND HE COULDN'T PAY FOR IT--I ALWAYS HELP MY FRIENDS OUT.

DENIAL OF THE VICTIM: THE PERSON ARGUES THAT THE VICTIMIZATION WAS DESERVED; THUS IT WAS NOT WRONG GIVEN THE CIRCUMSTANCES.

THE OWNER OF THIS STORE IS CROOKED ANYWAY--DO YOU SEE HOW MUCH HE CHARGES FOR COKES AT THE SODA FOUNTAIN?

DENIAL OF INJURY: THE PERSON ARGUES THAT THEIR ACTIONS DIDN'T HARM ANYONE.

IT'S NOT LIKE WHAT I DID HURT ANYONE. AND THIS IS A BIG STORE--THEY HAVE INSURANCE. WHAT'S ONE COMIC TO A BIG STORE?

THE FIVE TECHNIQUES OF NEUTRALIZATION ARE:

DENIAL OF RESPONSIBILITY: PEOPLE CLAIM THAT DUE TO OUTSIDE FORCES, THEY AREN'T RESPONSIBLE FOR THEIR BEHAVIOR.

OFFICER, I DIDN'T MEAN TO TAKE IT. I PUT IT IN MY POCKET AND FORGOT ABOUT IT.

THE 1950S SEEMED TO BE A TIME OF RELATIVE SOCIAL CONFORMITY.

DURING THIS PERIOD, TELEVISION SHOWS SUCH AS LEAVE IT TO BEAVER AND FATHER KNOWS BEST WERE ALMOST CARICATURES OF THE ERA...

...AND DESPITE THE FASCINATION WITH URBAN GANGS, YOUTH IN GENERAL WERE BEING CRITICIZED AS A MASS OF POP CULTURE CONFORMISTS.

AS THE 1960S PROGRESSED, HOWEVER, THINGS BEGAN TO CHANGE.

IMPORTANT SOCIAL, POLITICAL, AND CULTURAL EVENTS THAT TOOK PLACE IN THE UNITED STATES DURING THIS TIME HAD A CONSIDERABLE IMPACT ON CRIMINOLOGICAL THEORY.

FOR EXAMPLE, MANY SOCIAL AND POLITICAL MOVEMENTS EMERGED, EFFECTIVELY SHATTERING THE COMPLACENCY OF THE 1950S.

THERE WERE PROTESTS AGAINST THE VIETNAM WAR AND RIOTS IN MAJOR U.S. CITIES...

IMPORTANT LEADERS WERE ASSASSINATED AND CRIME RATES ROSE...

THESE AND OTHER DRAMATIC SOCIAL AND CULTURAL SHIFTS SEEMED TO SIGNAL THE COMPLETE BREAKDOWN OF PERSONAL AND SOCIAL CONTROL.

UNIVERSITY OF CALIFORNIA, BERKELEY, 1964.

THE TIMES WERE RIPE FOR THE EXPLORATION AND ACCEPTANCE OF A PERSPECTIVE THAT LINKED CRIME TO THE BREAKDOWN OF CONTROLS.

IN 1964, *TRAVIS HIRSCHI* WAS PURSUING HIS DOCTORATE AT THE UNIVERSITY OF CALIFORNIA, BERKELEY, A CENTER OF SOCIAL UNREST AT THIS TIME.

WHILE HE WAS THERE, HE HAD THE OPPORTUNITY TO WORK ON THE RICHMOND YOUTH PROJECT, A SELF-REPORT SURVEY OF 4,075 HIGH SCHOOL STUDENTS IN THE RICHMOND, CALIFORNIA, AREA.

IN EXCHANGE FOR HELPING OUT, HE WAS ALLOWED TO INCLUDE SOME ITEMS THAT HE WAS INTERESTED IN ON THE QUESTIONNAIRE.

HE SOON BECAME DIRECTOR OF THE PROJECT AND WAS RESPONSIBLE FOR THE DAY-TO-DAY COLLECTION OF THE SURVEY DATA.

IT WAS HARD WORK OVER THE COURSE OF SEVERAL MONTHS, BUT WHEN IT WAS FINISHED, HE HAD THE DATA HE NEEDED TO WRITE HIS DISSERTATION.

LAST ONE!

WHILE WORKING ON HIS DISSERTATION, HIRSCHI WAS HIRED AT UC BERKELEY AS AN ASSISTANT PROFESSOR FROM 1966 TO 1967.

IN 1967, HE MOVED TO THE UNIVERSITY OF WASHINGTON IN SEATTLE.

HEY--I JUST WANTED TO STOP BY AND WELCOME YOU TO THE DEPARTMENT, TRAVIS! WE HAVEN'T MET YET--I'M RON AKERS.*

HOW ARE YOU LIKING IT HERE?

THANKS! I HAVE TO SAY, IT SEEMS A LOT... QUIETER AROUND HERE.

AND NOT AS MUCH SUNSHINE...

*READ MORE ABOUT RONALD AKERS IN THE NEXT ISSUE, CRIMCOMICS: SOCIAL LEARNING THEORIES!

HAHA! BOTH TRUE STATEMENTS!

I'M GOING TO DINNER WITH ANOTHER COLLEAGUE, ROBERT BURGESS. WOULD YOU LIKE TO COME?

IN HIS THEORY, HIRSCHI IDENTIFIED FOUR SOCIAL BONDS: ATTACHMENT, COMMITMENT, INVOLVEMENT, AND BELIEF. THE STRONGER THE BOND, THE MORE LIKELY CRIMINAL BEHAVIOR IS CONTROLLED...THE WEAKER THE BOND, THE MORE LIKELY AN INDIVIDUAL WILL BREAK THE LAW.

ARE YOU EXCITED FOR TONIGHT, TOMMY?

YEAH, AND A LITTLE NERVOUS.

DON'T WORRY, SON. WE'LL BE THERE CHEERING YOU ON.

ATTACHMENT REFERS TO THE EMOTIONAL CLOSENESS YOUTHS HAVE WITH ADULTS, PARTICULARLY PARENTS. BEING CLOSE TO PARENTS MEANS THAT THERE IS WARM COMMUNICATION AND THE PARENTS KNOW WHAT THEY ARE UP TO.

YOUTHS DON'T WANT TO MISBEHAVE BECAUSE THEY CARE ABOUT THEIR PARENTS' OPINIONS AND DON'T WANT TO DISAPPOINT THEM. THIS CONTROLS YOUTHS' BEHAVIOR WHEN THE PARENTS AREN'T AROUND.

DARREN, YOU'RE GOING TO BE LATE FOR SCHOOL! MOM'S GOING TO BE REAL MAD!

WHATEVER.

COMMITMENT INVOLVES YOUTHS' STAKE IN CONFORMITY. THIS RELATES TO YOUTHS' HIGH EDUCATIONAL AND OCCUPATIONAL GOALS AND GETTING GOOD GRADES IN SCHOOL. THEY DON'T ENGAGE IN DELINQUENCY BECAUSE THEY DO NOT WANT TO RISK JEOPARDIZING THEIR COMMITMENTS.

DETENTION AGAIN, DARREN? THAT'S THE THIRD TIME THIS WEEK.

INVOLVEMENT REFERS TO PARTICIPATION IN CONVENTIONAL ACTIVITIES. IF YOUTHS SPEND THEIR TIME DOING HOMEWORK, PARTICIPATING IN SPORTS, OR DOING OTHER EXTRACURRICULAR ACTIVITIES, THEY WON'T HAVE TIME TO OFFEND.

IDLE HANDS ARE THE DEVIL'S WORKSHOP.

GOOD GAME TONIGHT, TOMMY!

THANK YOU, SIR.

BELIEF IS THE EXTENT TO WHICH YOUTHS EMBRACE THE MORAL VALIDITY OF THE LAW. CONFORMING YOUTH OBEY THE LAW BECAUSE THEY RESPECT IT AND SEE IT AS LEGITIMATE.

CRIME OCCURS WHEN CONVENTIONAL BELIEFS ARE WEAKENED. HIRSCHI BELIEVED THAT VARIATION IN THESE SOCIAL BONDS EXPLAINED VARIATION IN CRIME. THE BONDS ARE ALSO RELATED TO ONE ANOTHER: STRENGTH OR WEAKNESS IN ONE AFFECTS THE OTHERS.

CRIME PREVENTION TECHNIQUES BASED ON SOCIAL BOND THEORY COULD FOCUS ON PROGRAMS THAT INCREASE PARENT-CHILD ATTACHMENT OR FACILITATE ATTACHMENT AND COMMITMENT TO SCHOOL.

THE UNIVERSITY OF ARIZONA, 1990.

HIRSCHI LEFT THE UNIVERSITY OF WASHINGTON AND TAUGHT AT SEVERAL UNIVERSITIES BEFORE SETTLING AT THE UNIVERSITY OF ARIZONA.

IT WAS HERE HE COLLABORATED WITH *MICHAEL GOTTFREDSON*, AN INDIVIDUAL HE HAD MET WHEN THEY BOTH WERE AT THE STATE UNIVERSITY OF NEW YORK AT ALBANY.

WHILE AT ALBANY, THEY BEGAN TO COLLABORATE ON STUDIES OF SPECIFIC CORRELATES OF CRIME.

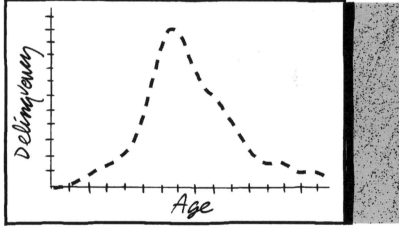

ONE OF THE CORRELATES WAS AGE, AND GOTTFREDSON AND HIRSCHI BEGAN TO SEE HOW THE CHARACTERISTICS OF THE *AGE-CRIME CURVE* COULD INFORM THEORY.

SO, THIS IS WHAT WE KNOW: THE AGE-CRIME CURVE IS INVARIANT AND CRIME DECLINES WITH AGE.

THESE BEHAVIORS BEGIN EARLY IN LIFE, NOT JUST ADOLESCENCE.

SO, THEORIES THAT FOCUS PRIMARILY ON THE PROCESSES AT OR ABOUT THE TEEN YEARS ARE, IN FACT, INCOMPLETE.

IN 1990, GOTTFREDSON AND HIRSCHI PUBLISHED A *GENERAL THEORY OF CRIME.* IN IT, THEY PROPOSED *SELF-CONTROL THEORY.*

GOTTFREDSON AND HIRSCHI SETTLED ON THE CONCEPT OF **SELF-CONTROL** IN ORDER TO DEVELOP A GENERAL THEORY THAT IDENTIFIED THE TENDENCY TO IGNORE COSTS IN FAVOR OF SHORT-TERM BENEFITS. SELF-CONTROL IS THE RESTRAINT THAT ALLOWS PEOPLE TO RESIST CRIME AND OTHER SHORT-TERM GRATIFICATION.

GOTTFREDSON AND HIRSCHI HYPOTHESIZED THAT LOW SELF-CONTROL IS THE RESULT OF INEFFECTIVE CHILD-REARING.

INEFFECTIVE PARENTING OCCURS WHEN PARENTS DO NOT MONITOR, RECOGNIZE, AND PUNISH DEVIANT BEHAVIOR.

ACCORDING TO GOTTFREDSON AND HIRSCHI, SELF-CONTROL STABILIZES BY THE TIME THE CHILD REACHES THE AGE OF EIGHT. THEREFORE, THE LEVEL OF SELF-CONTROL IS STABLE OVER THE LIFE COURSE, AND WILL AFFECT VIRTUALLY EVERY ASPECT OF A PERSON'S LIFE.

THE LOWER A PERSON'S SELF-CONTROL, THE HIGHER HIS INVOLVEMENT IN CRIMINAL AND ANALOGOUS BEHAVIORS.

ANALOGOUS BEHAVIORS INCLUDE THINGS LIKE SMOKING, DRINKING, GAMBLING, INVOLVEMENT IN ACCIDENTS, SEXUAL PROMISCUITY, AND OTHER PROBLEMATIC BEHAVIORS THAT MAY OR MAY NOT BE LEGALLY CATEGORIZED AS "CRIME."

PEOPLE WITH LOW SELF-CONTROL TEND TO BE "IMPULSIVE, INSENSITIVE, PHYSICAL (AS OPPOSED TO MENTAL), RISK-TAKING, SHORT-SIGHTED, AND NON-VERBAL."

GOTTFREDSON AND HIRSCHI CLAIM THAT SELF-CONTROL THEORY "EXPLAINS ALL CRIME, AT ALL TIMES, AND, FOR THAT MATTER, MANY FORMS OF BEHAVIOR THAT ARE NOT SANCTIONED BY THE STATE."

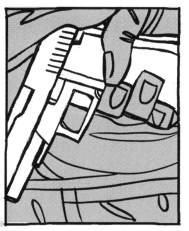

THEY ALSO CLAIM THAT THAT ALL CRIME CAN BE EXPLAINED AS A COMBINATION OF CRIMINAL OPPORTUNITY AND LOW SELF-CONTROL.

EMPIRICAL TESTS OF SELF-CONTROL THEORY GENERALLY SUPPORT THE THEORY'S CONCLUSION THAT LOW SELF-CONTROL IS RELATED TO CRIMINAL INVOLVEMENT.

TRAVIS HIRSCHI SET FORTH TWO OF THE MOST IMPORTANT CONTROL MODELS OF CRIME: SOCIAL BOND THEORY AND SELF-CONTROL THEORY (WITH MICHAEL GOTTFREDSON).

FOR MANY, IT IS PUZZLING AS TO WHY HIRSCHI CHANGED HIS VIEW ON THE SOURCE OF CONTROL.

HE ONCE THOUGHT THAT THE QUALITY OF SOCIAL BONDS DETERMINED THE LEVEL OF CRIME.

LATER, HE (WITH GOTTFREDSON) CAME TO BELIEVE THAT THE QUALITY OF SOCIAL BONDS AND THE LEVEL OF CRIME WERE BOTH CAUSED BY THE LEVEL OF SELF-CONTROL.

WITH RESPECT TO PREVENTION, BOTH OF THESE CONTROL THEORIES PROVIDE CONSIDERABLE SUPPORT FOR PROGRAMS TO STRENGTHEN FAMILIES, PARTICULARLY WITH RESPECT TO EFFECTIVE PARENTING.

PREVENTATIVE EFFORTS COULD TAKE THE FORM OF PARENTING CLASSES OR *EARLY INTERVENTION PROGRAMS.*

FOR ADULTS, HOWEVER, SOME HELPFUL PROGRAMS--ONES THAT FACILITATE STABLE SOCIAL NETWORKS OF EMPLOYMENT AND COMMUNITY ACTIVITIES--HAVE TENDED TO BE UNDERUTILIZED IN THE CURRENT "GET TOUGH" ERA.

IDEAS CAUSE REACTIONS.

SORRY, MA. SOMETIMES...I JUST CAN'T HELP MYSELF.

I KNOW... THAT'S WHAT YOU ALWAYS SAY...

THIS ISSUE EXPLORED THE DEVELOPMENT OF SOCIAL CONTROL THEORIES. WHILE MOST CRIMINOLOGICAL THEORIES ASK WHY INDIVIDUALS COMMIT CRIME, SOCIAL CONTROL THEORIES ASK A DIFFERENT QUESTION: "WHY DO PEOPLE CONFORM?" THIS STEMS FROM THE BELIEF THAT WHEN CONTROLS ARE PRESENT, CRIME DOES NOT OCCUR; WHEN CONTROLS ARE ABSENT, CRIME OFTEN OCCURS. THERE ARE SEVERAL CONTROL THEORIES COVERED IN THIS ISSUE.

WALTER RECKLESS'S CONTAINMENT THEORY FOCUSES ON AN INNER CONTROL SYSTEM AND AN OUTER CONTROL SYSTEM. ACCORDING THIS THEORY, THERE ARE INNER AND OUTER PUSHES AND PULLS THAT MAY PRODUCE DELINQUENCY UNLESS THEY ARE CONSTRAINED OR COUNTERACTED BY INNER AND OUTER CONTAINMENT MEASURES. OUTER CONTAINMENT IS THE SOCIAL ENVIRONMENT IN WHICH THE INDIVIDUAL LIVES AND REFLECTS COMMUNITY SOCIALIZATION. INNER CONTAINMENT CONTROLS THE INDIVIDUAL NO MATTER HOW THE EXTERNAL ENVIRONMENT MAY CHANGE.

GRESHAM SYKES AND DAVID MATZA ARGUED THAT WHILE DELINQUENTS RETAINED A COMMITMENT TO CONVENTIONAL SOCIETY AND ITS EXPECTATIONS, THEY COULD ENGAGE IN DELINQUENCY IF THEY COULD "ESCAPE" THE CONTROL THAT CONVENTIONAL SOCIETY HAD OVER THEM BY "NEUTRALIZING" THEIR VALUES TEMPORARILY. THESE TECHNIQUES OF NEUTRALIZATION INCLUDE DENIAL OF RESPONSIBILITY, DENIAL OF INJURY, DENIAL OF THE VICTIM, APPEAL TO HIGHER LOYALTIES, AND CONDEMNATION OF THE CONDEMNERS. LATER, DAVID MATZA WOULD EXPAND UPON THE NEUTRALIZATION TECHNIQUES AND PROPOSE THAT DELINQUENTS DON'T ENGAGE IN DELINQUENCY ALL THE TIME--THEY DRIFT BACK AND FORTH BETWEEN CONVENTIONAL AND DELINQUENT BEHAVIOR.

TRAVIS HIRSCHI IS CONSIDERED TO BE ONE OF THE MOST INFLUENTIAL CRIMINOLOGISTS OF OUR TIME. IN 1969, HE PUBLISHED CAUSES OF DELINQUENCY IN WHICH HE PUT FORTH SOCIAL BOND THEORY. IN HIS THEORY, HIRSCHI IDENTIFIED FOUR SOCIAL BONDS: ATTACHMENT, COMMITMENT, INVOLVEMENT, AND BELIEF. THE STRONGER THE BOND, THE MORE LIKELY CRIMINAL BEHAVIOR IS CONTROLLED; THE WEAKER THE BOND, THE MORE LIKELY AN INDIVIDUAL WILL BREAK THE LAW.

TWO DECADES LATER, HIRSCHI, ALONG WITH MICHAEL GOTTFREDSON, WOULD PUBLISH A SECOND CONTROL THEORY: SELF-CONTROL THEORY. SELF-CONTROL IS THE RESTRAINT THAT ALLOWS PEOPLE TO RESIST CRIME AND OTHER SHORT-TERM GRATIFICATION. PEOPLE WITH LOW SELF-CONTROL TEND TO BE "IMPULSIVE, INSENSITIVE, PHYSICAL (AS OPPOSED TO MENTAL), RISK-TAKING, SHORT-SIGHTED, AND NON-VERBAL." THEY HYPOTHESIZED THAT LOW SELF-CONTROL IS THE RESULT OF INEFFECTIVE CHILD-REARING. SELF-CONTROL STABILIZES BY THE TIME THE CHILD REACHES THE AGE OF EIGHT. THE LOWER A PERSON'S SELF-CONTROL, THE HIGHER HIS INVOLVEMENT IN CRIMINAL AND ANALOGOUS BEHAVIORS. THEY ALSO CLAIM THAT THAT ALL CRIME CAN BE EXPLAINED AS A COMBINATION OF CRIMINAL OPPORTUNITY AND LOW SELF-CONTROL.

Key Terms

Social Control Theories
Walter Reckless
Robert Park
Ernest Burgess
Chicago School
Social Psychology
Baby Boom
Albert J. Reiss
Jackson Toby
F. Ivan Nye
Containment Theory
Pushes
Pulls
Outer Containment
Inner Containment
Self-Concept
Goal Orientation
Frustration Tolerance
Norm Retention
Gresham Sykes

David Matza
Techniques of Neutralization
Denial of Responsibility
Denial of Injury
Denial of the Victim
Appeal to Higher Loyalties
Condemnation of the Condemners
Drift
Travis Hirschi
Social Bond Theory
Attachment
Commitment
Involvement
Belief
Michael Gottfredson
Age-Crime Curve
Self-Control Theory
Self-Control
Early Intervention Programs

Discussion Questions

1) Elaborate on the contributions of Albert Reiss, Jackson Toby, and F. Ivan to the development of control theory. What did their theories propose?

2) Explain how each of the five techniques of neutralization could be used to justify speeding.

3) How does control theory differ from strain theory and cultural deviance (i.e., differential association) theory?

4) What are the four social bonds? How does each help to control a youth from engaging in delinquency?

5) Compare and contrast Hirschi's social bond theory with Gottfredson and Hirschi's self-control theory.

Suggested Readings

Cullen, F. T., Agnew, R., & Wilcox, P. (2014). *Criminological theory: Past to present* (5th ed.). New York: Oxford University Press.

Gottfredson, M., & Hirschi, T. (1990). *A general theory of crime.* Stanford, CA: Stanford University Press.

Hirschi, T. (2002). *Causes of delinquency.* New York: Taylor & Francis.

Lilly, J. R., Cullen, F. T., & Ball, R. (2018). *Criminological theory: Context and consequences* (7th ed.). Los Angeles: Sage Publications.

Matza, D. (1964). *Delinquency and drift.* New York: Wiley.

Reckless, W. (1961). A new theory of delinquency and crime. *Federal Probation, 25,* 42–46.

Sykes, G., & Matza, D. (1957). Techniques of neutralization: A theory of delinquency. *American Sociological Review, 22,* 664–670.